ABOUT AUTHOR

Kamlesh Vishwakarma: A Visionary in Technology, Social Media, and E-Commerce -

Kamlesh Vishwakarma is a seasoned professional with over 24 years of experience across the dynamic domains of technology, social media, and e-commerce. His career reflects a profound commitment to innovation, growth, and the empowerment of businesses in the digital era.

What Is Social Media?

Social media refers to online platforms and applications that enable people to create, share, and interact with content, as well as connect and communicate with others. It facilitates the exchange of ideas, information, and experiences through various formats, including text, images, videos, and live streams.

Here's a list of popular social media platforms, categorized by their main features:

General Social Networking Platforms

1. **Facebook** – Connect with friends, family, and communities, share updates, photos, and events.
2. **LinkedIn** – Professional networking and career development.
3. **Twitter** – Share short messages (tweets), engage in public discussions, and follow trends.
4. **Mastodon** – Decentralized social network, similar to Twitter, with user-controlled communities.

Photo and Video Sharing Platforms

1. **Instagram** – Share photos, videos, and stories; focuses on visual content.
2. **Snapchat** – Send photos and videos that disappear after viewing; includes stories and filters.
3. **TikTok** – Short-form video content, music, and challenges, widely popular among younger users.

4. **YouTube** – Video sharing platform for entertainment, tutorials, vlogs, and more.
5. **Pinterest** – Visual discovery and bookmarking platform, focused on inspiration (e.g., crafts, fashion, recipes).

Messaging and Communication Platforms

1. **WhatsApp** – Instant messaging app for text, voice, and video calls.
2. **Messenger (by Facebook)** – Messaging service linked to Facebook for text and video chats.
3. **Telegram** – Cloud-based messaging with an emphasis on privacy and group communication.
4. **Discord** – Originally for gamers, now used for general communication, voice chats, and communities.
5. **Slack** – Primarily for business communication with channels, direct messaging, and file sharing.

Live Streaming and Interactive Platforms

1. **Twitch** – Live streaming platform, primarily for gaming and interactive content.
2. **YouTube Live** – Live streaming feature on YouTube for events, concerts, and personal streams.
3. **Facebook Live** – Live video broadcasting integrated with Facebook.
4. **Instagram Live** – Live streaming feature within Instagram for real-time engagement.

Interest-Based and Niche Communities

1. **Reddit** – Community-based platform where users can join "subreddits" to discuss specific topics.
2. **Quora** – Q&A platform where users ask questions and share answers.
3. **Nextdoor** – Social networking for neighborhoods, sharing local news and community updates.
4. **Goodreads** – Platform for book lovers to rate, review, and discuss books.
5. **Meetup** – Connect with people who share similar interests, hobbies, or professional goals.

Professional Networking and Job Search Platforms

1. **LinkedIn** – Social networking for professionals to connect, share career insights, and find job opportunities.
2. **Indeed** – Primarily a job search engine, with community features for reviews and career advice.

Creative Content Sharing

1. **Flickr** – Photo sharing and storage, often used by photographers for portfolio display.
2. **Behance** – Showcase for creative portfolios, especially in design, photography, and art.

Social Commerce

1. **Instagram Shopping** – A feature within Instagram that allows users to shop directly from posts and stories.

2. **TikTok Shopping** – A social commerce feature for discovering and purchasing products directly within the app.

Other Social Media Platforms

1. **Vero** – Ad-free, chronological feed platform focusing on visual content.
2. **Clubhouse** – Audio-based social network where users can participate in live discussions on various topics.
3. **Snapchat Spotlight** – A feature of Snapchat for short, viral videos.
4. **WeChat** – Popular in China for messaging, social networking, and mobile payments.

These platforms cater to different interests, from professional networking and creative sharing to live streaming and niche communities. Would you like to know more about a specific platform?

Impacts of Social Media in Our Society

Social media has significantly shaped modern society, bringing both positive and negative impacts across various aspects of life. Here's an overview:

Positive Impacts

1. **Enhanced Communication and Connectivity**
   - Social media enables people to connect across geographical boundaries, fostering global relationships.
   - It provides real-time updates and easy communication with friends, family, and colleagues.
2. **Information Access and Awareness**
   - Platforms disseminate information rapidly, keeping users informed about world events.
   - They raise awareness on social, environmental, and political issues.
3. **Business and Marketing Opportunities**
   - Businesses use social media for branding, advertising, and customer engagement.
   - Entrepreneurs and small businesses benefit from reaching larger audiences without significant marketing budgets.
4. **Educational and Learning Resources**
   - Platforms like YouTube and LinkedIn provide free and paid learning resources.
   - Online communities support peer-to-peer learning and mentorship.
5. **Advocacy and Social Movements**

- Social media has fueled impactful movements, like #MeToo and #BlackLivesMatter.
- It amplifies voices from marginalized communities.

6. **Fostering Creativity and Self-Expression**
    - Individuals showcase talents in art, music, writing, and more.
    - It encourages collaboration among creative communities.

Negative Impacts

1. **Mental Health Concerns**
    - Social media can contribute to anxiety, depression, and low self-esteem due to comparison and cyberbullying.
    - Addiction to platforms often leads to reduced productivity and social isolation.
2. **Spread of Misinformation**
    - Fake news and unchecked information can lead to panic, confusion, or harmful actions.
    - Echo chambers and algorithms reinforce biased views.
3. **Privacy Issues**
    - Sharing personal information increases risks of identity theft and data misuse.
    - Platforms often face criticism over data security practices.
4. **Negative Effects on Youth**
    - Excessive screen time impacts physical health, sleep, and cognitive development in children.

- Unrealistic beauty standards lead to body image issues.

5. **Decline in Real-World Interactions**
    - Online communication may replace meaningful face-to-face connections.
    - It often reduces empathy and interpersonal skills.
6. **Polarization and Division**
    - Algorithms prioritize sensational content, intensifying political and social divides.
    - Online arguments often escalate conflicts.

Social media is a powerful tool that, when used mindfully, can bring immense benefits to society. However, addressing its drawbacks through education, regulatory measures, and ethical platform design is crucial for creating a balanced and healthier digital ecosystem.

Pros of Social Media for Child

Social media for child can provide several benefits when used responsibly and in a controlled environment. Here are some of the pros:

1. Boosts Creativity

- Platforms like **LEGO Life** and **PopJam** encourage child to create and share artwork, videos, and projects, fostering creativity and self-expression.
- Child can explore creative outlets like photography, video editing, and storytelling.

2. Builds Communication Skills

- Social media helps child learn how to communicate effectively in a digital age.
- Apps like **Messenger Child** allow child to interact with family and friends in a safe environment, building social skills.

3. Encourages Learning

- Educational content on platforms like **YouTube Kids** can spark curiosity and expand knowledge.
- Challenges and quizzes on apps like **Zigazoo** make learning interactive and fun.

4. Fosters Connections

- Helps child stay connected with friends and relatives, especially those who live far away.
- Provides a sense of belonging as they engage with peers who share similar interests.

5. Promotes Digital Literacy

- Early exposure to social media can teach child how to navigate the digital world safely.
- They can learn about online etiquette, responsible sharing, and critical thinking when evaluating content.

6. Encourages Teamwork and Collaboration

- Child can work together on projects or join groups focused on shared interests, fostering teamwork.
- Platforms with group challenges help develop collaborative skills.

7. Provides Entertainment

- Age-appropriate games, videos, and challenges keep child entertained in a constructive way.
- Helps develop hobbies and discover passions through diverse content.

8. Teaches Responsibility

- Managing a social media account teaches child about setting boundaries, handling feedback, and the importance of online privacy.
- Parents can use it as a tool to instill responsible online behavior.

9. Sparks Inspiration

- Child can get inspired by others' creations or achievements and use that motivation to pursue their own goals.
- Exposure to diverse cultures and ideas can broaden their perspectives.

10. Builds Confidence

- Receiving positive feedback on their creations or ideas can boost child' self-esteem.
- Provides a platform for child to showcase their talents in a supportive community.

When guided and monitored properly, social media can be a valuable tool for child to grow, learn, and connect in a digital world. Would you like help with introducing safe platforms or setting rules for usage?

Cons of Social Media for Child

While social media for child has benefits, it also comes with potential downsides that parents should be aware of. Here's a breakdown of the cons:

1. Exposure to Inappropriate Content

- Despite age filters and moderation, child may still encounter unsuitable or harmful content.
- Algorithms can sometimes recommend age-inappropriate material.

2. Risk of Cyberbullying

- Child may experience or witness bullying online, which can harm their self-esteem and emotional well-being.
- Platforms with social interactions can sometimes foster negative comments or exclusion.

3. Privacy Concerns

- Child might share personal information unknowingly, putting their safety at risk.
- Some platforms collect user data, raising concerns about how it is used.

4. Addiction and Excessive Screen Time

- Social media can be highly engaging, leading to excessive usage and less time for physical activities, homework, or family interactions.
- Overuse can affect sleep patterns and overall health.

5. Unrealistic Comparisons

- Child might compare themselves to idealized or filtered images, leading to body image issues or reduced self-confidence.
- They may struggle with the pressure to gain likes, followers, or validation.

6. Distraction from Real-Life Activities

- Spending too much time online can detract from hobbies, outdoor play, and face-to-face socialization.
- It may affect academic performance if not managed well.

7. Risk of Predators

- Online platforms, even kid-friendly ones, can sometimes be exploited by individuals with harmful intentions.
- Interactions with strangers, if not properly monitored, can pose risks.

8. Exposure to Ads and Consumerism

- Many platforms display targeted ads, potentially influencing child to want unnecessary products or fostering materialistic attitudes.
- They may not yet have the critical thinking skills to differentiate between content and advertisements.

9. Emotional Stress

- Child may feel stress or anxiety from maintaining an online presence or dealing with negative interactions.
- Fear of missing out (FOMO) can develop if they see others participating in activities they aren't involved in.

10. Dependence on Validation

- Constantly seeking approval through likes, comments, or followers can make child overly dependent on external validation.
- This can lead to anxiety or a sense of inadequacy when expectations are not met.

11. Lack of Regulation

- Some platforms may lack sufficient moderation or fail to enforce rules, leading to inappropriate interactions or content slipping through.

12. Reduced Critical Thinking

- Constant exposure to short, entertaining content can impact child' attention spans and critical thinking skills.
- They may become more reactive than reflective in their interactions.

How to Mitigate the Cons

1. **Parental Monitoring:** Regularly check your child's activity and discuss their online experiences.
2. **Educate About Risks:** Teach child about privacy, recognizing harmful content, and how to report issues.
3. **Set Limits:** Establish clear boundaries for screen time and social media usage.
4. **Use Kid-Friendly Platforms:** Opt for platforms specifically designed for children, which offer stricter safety measures.

Would you like suggestions on balancing these risks or tips on setting up parental controls?

How Social Media Affecting Child

Social media has transformed how we connect and communicate, but it also poses challenges, especially for children. Here are some ways social media can negatively affect child:

1. Mental Health Issues

- **Increased Anxiety and Depression:** Exposure to filtered, idealized versions of life can lead to feelings of inadequacy, low self-esteem, and anxiety.
- **Fear of Missing out (FOMO):** Constant updates about others' activities can make child feel excluded or left out, triggering stress.

2. Cyberbullying

- Social media provides platforms for bullying, which can be persistent and anonymous. Victims may face emotional trauma, which affects their overall well-being.

3. Addiction and Overuse

- Many child struggle to regulate their screen time. Excessive use can lead to social media addiction, disrupting daily activities like studying, exercising, and sleeping.

4. Sleep Disruption

- Nighttime use of social media can interfere with sleep due to screen exposure and the compulsion to stay updated, impacting health and cognitive functions.

5. Distorted Body Image

- Seeing unrealistic beauty standards on social media can lead to body dissatisfaction, eating disorders, and unhealthy comparison behaviors.

6. Privacy Concerns

- Child may unknowingly share too much personal information, making them vulnerable to online predators, scams, or identity theft.

7. Exposure to Harmful Content

- Social media may expose children to inappropriate content, including violence, self-harm, or harmful ideologies, which can negatively influence their behavior or thinking.

8. Impaired Social Skills

- Excessive virtual interactions might reduce opportunities for real-life socialization, impairing the development of crucial communication and interpersonal skills.

9. Reduced Academic Performance

- Constant notifications and the lure of social media can distract child from their studies, leading to procrastination and lower academic achievement.

10. Unrealistic Expectations

- Social media can create unrealistic expectations for relationships, achievements, and lifestyles, leading to frustration and disappointment.

Tips for Parents to Mitigate These Effects

- **Set Time Limits:** Enforce screen-time restrictions to ensure a healthy balance.
- **Monitor Activity:** Be aware of the platforms your child uses and their interactions.
- **Encourage Open Communication:** Foster an environment where your child feels comfortable discussing online experiences.
- **Educate About Privacy:** Teach your child the importance of protecting personal information.
- **Promote Offline Activities:** Encourage hobbies, sports, and family time to reduce dependence on screens.
- **Lead by Example:** Model responsible social media use yourself.

By staying involved and informed, parents can help their child navigate the digital world more safely and healthily.

Teaching Child to Be Smart About Social Media

Teaching child to be smart about social media is crucial for their safety and well-being. Here are some strategies to help guide them:

1. Set Clear Guidelines and Boundaries

- **Age Appropriateness:** Set an age-appropriate limit for when child can start using social media. Many platforms require users to be at least 13 years old, but even then, it's important to discuss the risks and ensure they understand the responsibilities.
- **Screen Time Limits:** Establish daily or weekly screen time limits to ensure they balance social media use with other important activities, such as schoolwork, family time, and sleep.

2. Teach Them about Privacy

- **Personal Information:** Teach child not to share personal details (e.g., home address, phone number, or school) online. Emphasize the importance of privacy settings and how to adjust them to control who can see their posts.
- **Safe Sharing:** Help them understand the risks of posting photos or videos that could be misused or seen by people they don't know.

3. Discuss the Risks of Cyberbullying

- **Recognizing Bullying:** Help child understand what cyberbullying is and how it can affect others. Encourage them to speak up if they witness or experience bullying online.
- **Responding to Bullying:** Discuss strategies for handling bullying, such as blocking or reporting the bully and speaking to an adult for support.

4. Promote Critical Thinking

- **Questioning Content:** Teach child to critically evaluate content on social media. Remind them that not everything online is true or authentic, and to be cautious of influencers, ads, and viral trends.
- **Avoiding Peer Pressure:** Empower children to resist the pressure to conform to online trends, especially those that promote unhealthy behaviors or unrealistic standards.

5. Encourage Respectful and Positive Interaction

- **Kindness Online:** Discuss the importance of being kind, respectful, and empathetic in their online interactions. Encourage positive engagement and discourage negative behaviors such as trolling or spreading hate.
- **Digital Footprint:** Help them to understand that everything they post online contributes to their digital footprint, which can last forever and impact their future.

6. Model Responsible Social Media Use

- **Set an Example:** Children often imitate their parents. Be a role model by demonstrating healthy social media habits. Show them how to use social media responsibly, prioritize real-world relationships, and balance screen time.
- **Discuss Your Online Life:** Share how you stay safe online, the boundaries you set for your own social media use, and how you manage privacy settings.

7. Foster Open Communication

- **Encourage Open Dialogue:** Create a safe space where your child feel comfortable talking to you about their online experiences, whether it's about something troubling or exciting.
- **Stay Informed:** Be aware of the social media platforms they are using and the trends within their peer group. Keep the lines of communication open so you can address any concerns before they become larger issues.

8. Teach Them to Handle Negative Feedback

- **Dealing with Criticism:** Teach your child how to respond to negative comments or feedback online, emphasizing that they should not take it personally and should consider the source before reacting.
- **Self-Confidence:** Help them build resilience so they don't feel pressured by online criticism, focusing on building their self-worth outside of social media.

9. Encourage Offline Activities

- **Balance with Real-World Interaction:** Encourage participation in offline hobbies, sports, and social activities that don't involve screens. A well-rounded lifestyle helps prevent overreliance on social media for validation or entertainment.
- **Outdoor Time and Family Connection:** Prioritize family time and outdoor activities that don't involve technology to foster real-life connections.

10. Utilize Parental Controls and Monitoring Tools

- **Use Parental Controls:** Take advantage of the parental control features that many platforms offer to monitor and limit your child's social media use.
- **Monitor Activity:** While it's important to respect privacy, you can also occasionally check their social media accounts (with respect to their boundaries) to ensure they are staying safe.

Teaching child to be smart about social media involves a balance of open communication, education, and modeling healthy habits. By providing them with the tools to navigate the online world responsibly, you help them enjoy the benefits of social media while minimizing the risks.

Social Media and School Studies

Social media can have both positive and negative effects on school studies, depending on how it is used. Here are some of the ways it can impact students' academic performance:

Positive Effects:

1. **Access to Information**: Social media platforms like YouTube, LinkedIn, and Facebook groups offer educational content, tutorials, and resources. Students can connect with experts, watch instructional videos, and access learning materials that may not be available in textbooks.
2. **Collaboration and Networking**: Social media can enable students to collaborate with peers on projects, share ideas, and help each other with studies. Platforms like Google Classroom, Slack, or even WhatsApp groups allow for easy communication and collaboration on assignments or group work.
3. **Inspiration and Motivation**: Following educational influencers or joining academic communities on platforms like Instagram, Twitter, or TikTok can motivate students. They can gain insights into study habits, career paths, and ways to improve their academic skills.
4. **Building Soft Skills**: Through social media interactions, students can develop skills like communication, digital literacy, and networking that are valuable in the modern workforce.

Negative Effects:

1. **Distraction**: Social media can be a major source of distraction. Notifications, chats, and endless scrolling through posts can take students' attention away from their studies. This often results in procrastination and reduced focus on academic tasks.
2. **Reduced Academic Performance**: Studies have shown that excessive use of social media can be linked to lower academic performance. Time spent on social media often cuts into study time, and it can affect sleep patterns, leading to fatigue and poor concentration during class.
3. **Mental Health Issues**: Social media can contribute to stress, anxiety, and depression among students, particularly when they compare themselves to others or experience cyberbullying. Mental health issues can significantly affect academic performance and overall well-being.
4. **Decreased Face-to-Face Interaction**: Excessive use of social media can reduce in-person interactions and communication skills. This might affect students' ability to engage in classroom discussions, participate in group activities, or develop interpersonal skills.
5. **Misinformation**: Students may encounter unreliable or biased information on social media, which could impact their understanding of subjects. It becomes essential for students to develop critical thinking and media literacy skills to differentiate between credible and false information.

How to Balance Social Media Use and School Studies:

- **Set Time Limits**: Students can set time limits for social media usage, such as during breaks, to avoid getting distracted during study time.
- **Use Social Media for Learning**: By following educational pages, joining study groups, or using platforms like YouTube for tutorials, social media can become a helpful tool for enhancing academic knowledge.
- **Practice Digital Detox**: Taking regular breaks from social media, especially during exam periods or while working on assignments, can help students focus better.
- **Parental Supervision and Guidance**: For younger students, it's essential for parents to monitor social media use and ensure that it doesn't interfere with academic goals.

In conclusion, social media has the potential to both enhance and hinder academic success. It's important for students to find a healthy balance and use it effectively for learning while avoiding the negative distractions that can arise from excessive use.

Law for Cyberbullying

Cyberbullying is a growing concern, and many countries have implemented laws to address and prevent it. These laws vary depending on the country or state, but the general aim is to provide protection for individuals who are subjected to online harassment and to hold perpetrators accountable. Below are some key points regarding laws for cyberbullying in different regions:

United States:

In the U.S., there is no single federal law specifically targeting cyberbullying. However, various states have passed their own laws to address online harassment. Key features include:

1. **State Laws**: Each state has its own set of laws related to cyberbullying. As of recent years, all 50 states have enacted some form of anti-bullying laws, and many have expanded them to include cyberbullying. These laws typically cover harassment, threats, and other forms of harmful online behavior.
2. **The Communications Decency Act (CDA) - Section 230**: While this law grants immunity to internet service providers from liability for content posted by users, it doesn't prevent state or federal laws from prosecuting cyberbullying. However, this can make it difficult to pursue action against platforms that allow cyberbullying to occur.
3. **Federal Laws**: In some cases, federal laws may apply to cyberbullying, especially if the harassment involves

interstate communications. The **Federal Hate Crimes Act** or **stalking laws** can sometimes be used to prosecute cyberbullying incidents, especially if the harassment is severe, targeted, or involves threats of violence.

4. **Schools and Cyberbullying**: The **Violence against Women Act** and other education laws give schools the authority to take action against bullying, including cyberbullying, if it interferes with a student's right to receive an education.

United Kingdom:

The UK has a number of laws that can be applied to cases of cyberbullying:

1. **The Malicious Communications Act 1988**: This law makes it an offense to send communications (including messages, social media posts, or emails) that are indecent, offensive, or threatening. If cyberbullying involves harassment or threats, this law can be used to prosecute offenders.
2. **The Protection from Harassment Act 1997**: This law can be used when cyberbullying involves repeated behavior that causes alarm or distress. It can be used in cases of online stalking or repeated harassment.
3. **The Communications Act 2003**: This law can be used to prosecute individuals who send messages that are grossly offensive or obscene.
4. **The Defamation Act 2013**: If cyberbullying involves defamation or spreading false information online that

harms someone's reputation, the defamation laws in the UK can be applied.

5. **The Children's Online Privacy Protection Act (COPPA)**: Although this U.S. law specifically applies to children under 13, it prohibits the collection of personal information from minors online and aims to protect them from online harassment.

Canada:

Canada has both federal and provincial laws that address cyberbullying:

1. **Criminal Code of Canada**: Cyberbullying can fall under harassment, criminal defamation, and uttering threats. For example, section 264 of the Criminal Code addresses criminal harassment, which includes stalking and online threats.
2. **The Anti-Cyberbullying Act**: Passed in 2013, this law makes it easier for victims of cyberbullying to seek a court order to remove harmful material from the internet.
3. **Provincial Laws**: Some provinces, like Ontario, have implemented laws aimed at preventing and addressing cyberbullying in schools. For example, Ontario's **Education Act** requires schools to take action against bullying, including cyberbullying, and implement anti-bullying policies.

Australia:

Australia has several laws to combat cyberbullying:

1. **Criminal Code Act 1995**: Cyberbullying involving threats, harassment, or stalking can fall under various provisions of the Criminal Code, such as those dealing with stalking, threats of violence, and using a carriage service (like the internet) to menace, harass, or cause offense.
2. **The Enhancing Online Safety Act 2015**: This law established the **Office of the eSafety Commissioner**, which works to promote online safety, including tackling cyberbullying. It allows individuals to report harmful online content and provides the eSafety Commissioner with the power to issue removal notices to social media platforms.
3. **Cyberbullying in Schools**: Australian states like New South Wales and Victoria have passed laws requiring schools to develop and implement anti-bullying policies, including addressing cyberbullying.

General Principles of Cyberbullying Laws:

Cyberbullying laws generally cover several key areas:

- **Harassment**: Repeated online behavior that causes distress, fear, or alarm.
- **Defamation**: Spreading false information online that harms a person's reputation.
- **Threats of Violence**: Threatening harm or violence, including physical threats, sexual threats, or threats of damage to property.
- **Stalking**: Using online platforms to track or follow someone obsessively.

- **Public Humiliation**: Posting embarrassing or harmful content online to humiliate or degrade the victim.
- **Children's Protection**: Laws that specifically aim to protect minors from online harassment, including restrictions on the sharing of explicit or harmful content.

India

In India, cyberbullying is addressed under various legal provisions that focus on online harassment, defamation, and the misuse of technology. While there isn't a specific law dedicated solely to cyberbullying, there are several laws under the Indian Penal Code (IPC) and other legislations that can be used to address and punish those involved in cyberbullying. Here's an overview of the key laws related to cyberbullying in India:

1. Indian Penal Code (IPC)

Several sections of the IPC can be invoked for cyberbullying, depending on the nature of the offense:

- **Section 354A (Sexual Harassment)**: This section criminalizes sexual harassment, including online harassment like sending obscene messages or videos. If cyberbullying involves unwelcome sexual advances or explicit content, this section can be applied.
- **Section 499 (Defamation)**: If the cyberbullying involves spreading false statements or defamatory content to damage someone's reputation, Section 499

can be used to prosecute the offender. The law covers both online and offline defamation.

- **Section 503 (Criminal Intimidation)**: If the cyberbullying involves threats of harm, injury, or violence, this section can be used. Threats made through electronic communication, like social media messages or emails, fall under this provision.
- **Section 506 (Punishment for Criminal Intimidation)**: This section deals with the punishment for criminal intimidation, including threats made through online platforms.
- **Section 507 (Criminal Intimidation by Anonymous Communication)**: If the cyberbullying is done anonymously, Section 507 allows punishment for anonymous communication used to intimidate or threaten the victim.
- **Section 509 (Word, Gesture, or Act Intended to Insult the Modesty of a Woman)**: This section can be applied if the cyberbullying is specifically targeting a woman and involves gestures, words, or acts that insult her modesty online.

2. Information Technology Act, 2000 (IT Act)

The **Information Technology Act, 2000** is a comprehensive legislation that deals with offenses related to cybercrime, including cyberbullying. Some key sections under the IT Act include:

- **Section 66A (Sending Offensive Messages through Communication Service, etc.)**: This section, which was initially used to prosecute people sending offensive or menacing messages through electronic communication, was struck down by the Supreme Court in 2015 due to concerns about free speech. However, similar actions may still be prosecuted under other sections of the IT Act.

- **Section 66C (Identity Theft)**: If the cyberbullying involves stealing someone's identity online or impersonating someone, this section can be used to address the offense. It criminalizes identity theft or using someone's personal information without authorization.
- **Section 66D (Cheating by Personation Using Computer Resources)**: If a person uses fake profiles, photographs, or information to deceive or harass others online, this section can be applied. It specifically targets fraudulent activities carried out online.
- **Section 67 (Publishing or Transmitting Obscene Material in Electronic Form)**: This section criminalizes the transmission or publication of obscene or sexually explicit content via electronic media, including social media platforms. Cyberbullying involving explicit material or "revenge porn" falls under this section.
- **Section 67A (Punishment for Publishing or Transmitting Material Containing Sexually Explicit Act)**: If cyberbullying involves sharing or publishing sexually explicit content without consent, this provision can be used to prosecute the offender.
- **Section 72 (Breach of Privacy)**: This section deals with the unauthorized disclosure of personal information obtained through electronic means, which can be

relevant if cyberbullying involves the sharing of private messages, images, or videos without consent.

3. Protection of Children from Sexual Offences (POCSO) Act, 2012

If the victim of cyberbullying is a child (below the age of 18), the **POCSO Act** can be applied, especially if the cyberbullying involves sexual content or exploitation. The Act provides protection against online sexual abuse, harassment, and exploitation of minors.

4. Cyberbullying and the Role of Social Media Platforms

Under the **Information Technology (Intermediary Guidelines and Digital Media Ethics Code) Rules, 2021**, social media platforms are required to take down content that promotes or facilitates cyberbullying. Social media companies like Facebook, Instagram, Twitter, and YouTube must comply with these rules by:

- Having a grievance redressal mechanism in place.
- Acting swiftly to remove harmful content within a specified time.
- Appointing a grievance officer to address complaints related to online harassment or bullying.

This provides a means for victims to report incidents of cyberbullying on these platforms, and the companies are legally bound to act.

5. Other Relevant Laws

- **The Juvenile Justice (Care and Protection of Children) Act, 2015**: This Act covers cases where minors are involved as either victims or perpetrators of cyberbullying. If a child or adolescent is the perpetrator, the Juvenile Justice Act may come into play, especially in cases of online abuse.
- **Revenge Pornography**: Although there is no separate law for "revenge porn" in India, it can be prosecuted under the existing provisions of the **IPC** (defamation and harassment) and the **IT Act** (publishing obscene content).

Challenges in Addressing Cyberbullying in India

- **Anonymity**: Perpetrators of cyberbullying often operate under fake identities, making it difficult to trace them and hold them accountable.
- **Jurisdiction**: Cyberbullying often occurs across borders, making it hard to enforce Indian laws in cases where the perpetrator is located in another country.
- **Awareness**: Many victims of cyberbullying may not be fully aware of their legal rights or the process to report cyberbullying incidents effectively.

Steps for Victims of Cyberbullying

1. **Report to the Platform**: Victims can report cyberbullying to social media platforms, which are required to act swiftly to remove offensive content.
2. **File a Complaint**: Victims can file a complaint with the local police or cybercrime cells. Many states in India

have specialized cybercrime cells to deal with online offenses.

3. **Take Legal Action**: If needed, victims can file a case under the relevant provisions of the IPC or the IT Act. They can also approach the courts for orders to remove defamatory or harmful content from the internet.
4. **Cyber Help Centers**: Several states in India have set up helplines and websites to help victims of cyberbullying report their cases and seek assistance.

Challenges in Enforcing Cyberbullying Laws:

- **Anonymity**: Cyberbullying often occurs anonymously, making it difficult to identify perpetrators.
- **Jurisdiction**: The global nature of the internet makes it difficult to enforce national laws when the perpetrator is in a different country.
- **Freedom of Speech**: Striking a balance between protecting individuals from harm while respecting free speech rights is a complex issue in cyberbullying cases.

Prevention and Education:

Many countries emphasize education and awareness programs, especially for schools, to help prevent cyberbullying. These programs focus on teaching students about responsible online behavior, the consequences of cyberbullying, and how to report incidents.

In conclusion, while there are laws in many countries to address cyberbullying, the challenge often lies in enforcement, especially across different jurisdictions. As online interactions continue to evolve, laws are likely to continue adapting to ensure the protection of individuals from online harm.

Digital Privacy Law

Digital privacy law refers to the body of laws and regulations that govern the collection, use, storage, and sharing of personal data in the digital realm. These laws aim to protect individuals' privacy and ensure that organizations handle personal data responsibly and securely. Digital privacy laws are important in the context of online activities such as browsing the internet, using social media, engaging in e-commerce, and interacting with digital devices.

Key aspects of digital privacy law include:

1. **Data Collection and Consent**: Laws often require organizations to obtain explicit consent from individuals before collecting their personal data.
2. **Data Protection**: Organizations are obligated to protect personal data from unauthorized access, breaches, or misuse.
3. **Right to Access and Control**: Individuals may have the right to access their data, request corrections, or delete it.
4. **Transparency**: Organizations are typically required to disclose how personal data is being used, stored, and shared.
5. **Cross-Border Data Transfers**: Laws regulate how personal data is transferred across borders, ensuring adequate protection in different countries.

These laws are evolving in response to the growing concerns over digital privacy, and they are increasingly important for both individuals and businesses in the digital age.

Blocking Internet Access and Website in Internet Wi-Fi Router

Steps to Block Websites in Router:

1. **Log into the Router Admin Page**:
    - Open a web browser on a device connected to your network.
    - Type your router's IP address into the address bar. Common router IP addresses include:
        - 192.168.0.1
        - 192.168.1.1
    - Press Enter.
    - You'll be prompted to enter a username and password. If you haven't changed them, they might still be the default (check your router's manual or sticker for this information).
2. **Find the Website Blocking Settings**:
    - After logging in, look for a section related to **Security, Access Restrictions, Parental Controls**, or **Firewall.**
    - Some routers may have a dedicated option for website filtering or blocking.
3. **Block Specific Websites**:
    - Once you've found the website blocking feature, there will usually be a field to enter the website URLs you wish to block.
    - Add the website addresses (e.g., www.example.com or example.com) to the list.
    - Some routers allow you to block websites by keywords, categories, or IP addresses.

4. **Apply and Save the Changes**:
    - After adding the websites you want to block, save or apply the changes.
    - The router might reboot automatically or require you to manually restart it.
5. **Test the Blocked Websites**:
    - Try to access the blocked websites from a device connected to your router. If everything was done correctly, the sites should be inaccessible.

Example with Popular Routers:

- **Netgear**:
    - Log in to the router.
    - Navigate to **Advanced > Security > Block Sites**.
    - Enter the websites you wish to block in the provided field.
- **TP-Link**:
    - Log in to the router.
    - Go to **Access Control**.
    - Enable it and configure rules to block websites by URL.
- **D-Link**:
    - Log in to the router.
    - Go to **Access Control** or **Parental Control**.
    - Add the websites to block.

Blocking Internet Access

Steps to Block Internet Access on Your Router:

1. **Log into the Router Admin Page**:
    - Open a web browser on a device connected to your network.
    - Type your router's IP address into the address bar. Common addresses include:
        - 192.168.0.1
        - 192.168.1.1
    - Press Enter.
    - Enter the router's username and password. If you haven't changed these, check your router's manual or the sticker on the device for default credentials.
2. **Find the Device List**:
    - After logging in, look for a section that displays a list of all connected devices. This might be under **Device Management**, **LAN Status**, **Attached Devices**, or **Connected Devices**.
    - The list shows the devices currently using your network, often by their MAC address, IP address, or device name.
3. **Choose the Device to Block**:
    - Identify the device(s) you want to block. You can usually identify them by the device name, MAC address, or IP address.
4. **Block Internet Access for Specific Device**:
    - Look for an option like **Access Control**, **MAC Filtering**, **Parental Controls**, or **Device Management**.

- Some routers have a feature called **Access Control** or **Blacklisting**, where you can block a specific device from accessing the internet.
- If your router has **MAC Filtering**, you can block or allow devices based on their MAC address. You can either blacklist the MAC address to block internet access or whitelist only specific devices to allow internet use.
- Some routers also allow you to schedule internet access for certain devices.

5. **Apply and Save the Changes**:
    - After selecting the device(s) and applying the internet-blocking rule, save the settings and reboot the router if necessary.
6. **Test the Connection**:
    - Check if the blocked device(s) can still connect to the internet. They should no longer have internet access.

Example with Popular Routers:

- **Netgear**:
    - Log in to the router.
    - Go to **Advanced > Security > Access Control**.
    - Enable **Access Control** and select **Block** for the devices you want to block.
- **TP-Link**:
    - Log in to the router.
    - Navigate to **Access Control** or **Parental Controls**.
    - Select the devices you want to block and set the action to block internet access.

- **D-Link**:
    - Log in to the router.
    - Go to **Access Control** or **Parental Control** settings.
    - Choose to block devices by their MAC address or schedule internet access.

Tools and Devices for Childs Online Safety

Ensuring online safety for child is a critical concern for parents, as it helps protect them from harmful content, cyberbullying, and online predators. Fortunately, there are several tools and devices designed to help manage and monitor online activities, giving parents more control over what their children access. Here are some key tools and devices for online safety:

1. Parental Control Software

Parental control software allows parents to monitor and limit what their children can do online, such as blocking inappropriate websites, setting time limits, and tracking activity.

- **Qustodio**: Offers web filtering, time management, and monitoring of social media activity. It also provides detailed reports on children's activity.

- **Norton Family**: Provides web filtering, time management, and location tracking. It helps you monitor and manage your child's online activity.
- **Net Nanny**: Offers content filtering, time management, and social media monitoring. It allows real-time alerts if suspicious activity is detected.
- **Kaspersky Safe Child**: Includes features like location tracking, app usage monitoring, and blocking inappropriate websites.
- **Circle with Disney**: This device connects to your home Wi-Fi network and allows you to manage screen time, filter content, and even pause the internet for specific devices.

2. Device-Specific Tools

Many devices come with built-in parental control features to monitor and manage screen time, app usage, and access to content.

- **iOS (Apple)**:
    - **Screen Time**: Apple's built-in feature to limit screen time, block apps, and control access to content based on age appropriateness.
    - **Family Sharing**: Allows parents to manage children's purchases, set up restrictions, and track their child' devices.
- **Android**:
    - **Google Family Link**: Lets parents set screen time limits, monitor app activity, and manage content restrictions. It also includes location tracking features.

    - **Samsung Child Mode**: Provides a safe environment for child to use their Samsung devices with restricted access to apps and content.
- **Amazon Fire Tablets**:
    - **Amazon Child+**: Offers a library of kid-friendly books, videos, apps, and games. It also includes time limits, activity reports, and website filtering.
    - **Parental Controls**: Manage device usage, control access to apps and content, and restrict purchases.

3. Web Filters and Safe Browsing Tools

These tools help block harmful content and ensure child only access age-appropriate websites.

- **OpenDNS FamilyShield**: A free DNS service that automatically blocks adult websites and provides safe browsing for children.
- **Google SafeSearch**: A feature that helps filter out explicit content from Google search results.
- **Bark**: A tool that monitors social media, text messages, and emails for potential dangers like cyberbullying, inappropriate content, or online predators. It also alerts parents when issues are detected.
- **CleanBrowsing**: A DNS-based filtering service that offers a safe browsing experience by blocking inappropriate content across devices.

4. Wi-Fi and Router Controls

Many modern routers come with features to control internet access, filter content, and set screen time limits.

- **Circle Home Plus**: A device that connects to your router to manage and monitor all devices on the home network. It includes features like content filtering, time limits, and reporting.
- **Google Nest Wi-Fi / Google Wi-Fi**: Offers robust parental controls, allowing you to pause the internet for certain devices, set time limits, and filter content by age.
- **TP-Link Deco**: Includes built-in parental controls for blocking harmful websites, setting internet usage schedules, and limiting access to certain devices.
- **Netgear Orbi**: Has advanced parental controls, allowing you to set time limits, filter websites, and monitor network activity.

5. Monitoring Apps

These apps provide real-time monitoring of a child's online activity, allowing parents to stay informed about their child's internet usage.

- **Life360**: A family safety app that includes location tracking, driving safety features, and geofencing. It also helps parents track their child's online interactions.
- **FamilyTime**: Offers GPS location tracking, app blocking, web filtering, and screen time management.

It also includes geofencing to notify parents when their child leave or arrive at certain locations.

- **OurPact**: Lets parents set screen time limits, block specific apps, and create a device schedule for child. It also offers geofencing and location tracking features.

6. Educational and Interactive Tools

Some apps and devices provide both safety features and educational content to help children learn about responsible online behavior.

- **Kiddle**: A search engine built specifically for child. It filters out inappropriate content and provides a safe environment for children to explore the web.
- **YouTube Child**: A child-friendly version of YouTube that includes a wide range of educational and entertaining videos while filtering out inappropriate content.
- **GizmoWatch**: A smartwatch designed for child with location tracking, emergency alerts, and the ability to make calls to preset contacts. It also helps monitor screen time and online activity.

7. Social Media Monitoring Tools

Social media is an area where child are often exposed to risks such as cyberbullying or inappropriate content. These tools help parents monitor activity on social media platforms.

- **Bark**: Monitors social media platforms for harmful behavior, cyberbullying, and inappropriate content. It provides parents with alerts and detailed reports.

- **Mspy**: A monitoring tool that tracks phone activities, including text messages, calls, social media apps, and web browsing history.

Combining a range of these tools can help ensure a comprehensive online safety strategy for children. It's important to engage with your child about online safety, set clear boundaries, and regularly check their online activity.

Google Parental Controls

Google provides robust parental control features for Android devices through **Google Family Link**, which helps manage your child's device usage and keep them safe online. Here's a step-by-step guide:

1. Set Up Google Family Link

For Parents:

1. **Download Family Link**:
    - Install the **Google Family Link for parents** app on your Android device from the Google Play Store.
2. **Create a Family Group**:
    - Open the app and follow prompts to create a Google Family Group.
    - Sign in with your Google account.
3. **Set Up Child's Account**:
    - If your child doesn't have a Google account, you can create one during setup.
    - If they already have an account, you'll link it to Family Link.

For Children:

4. **Install Family Link on Their Device**:
    - Install the **Google Family Link for children & teens** app on your child's Android device.
    - Follow the prompts to link their account to the parent's account.

5. **Grant Necessary Permissions**:
    - Allow Family Link to manage your child's device by enabling the requested permissions.

2. Customize Parental Controls

Once the setup is complete, you can manage the settings from the **Family Link for parents** app on your device:

Screen Time Management:

- Set daily screen time limits for apps and overall device use.
- Schedule "Bedtime" to restrict device usage during specific hours.

App Permissions:

- Approve or block apps your child tries to download from the Google Play Store.
- Set restrictions based on age ratings for apps, movies, books, and games.

Content Filtering:

- Enable SafeSearch to filter explicit content in Google searches.
- Turn on Restricted Mode on YouTube to limit access to inappropriate videos.

Location Tracking:

- View the real-time location of your child's device (if location sharing is enabled).

3. Monitor and Adjust Settings

Weekly Activity Reports:

- View detailed reports of how much time your child spends on each app or activity.

Remote Controls:

- Lock the device instantly when needed.
- Remotely change settings, such as screen time limits.

For more detailed guidance, visit Google Family Link Help. This tool empowers parents to manage their child's digital experience while promoting responsible online behavior.

Age Restriction on Social Media

Age Restrictions on Social Media are implemented to ensure that users have the maturity and capacity to engage responsibly with online content and interactions. Most platforms set their minimum age requirement at **13 years**, in compliance with laws such as the **Children's Online Privacy Protection Act (COPPA)** in the United States.

Standard Age Restrictions on Popular Platforms

- **Facebook, Instagram, Snapchat, TikTok, Twitter/X, and YouTube**: 13 years and older.
- **WhatsApp**:
    - **16 years or older** in some regions (e.g., Europe due to GDPR).
    - **13 years or older** in most other parts of the world.
- **LinkedIn**: 16 years and older.

Reasons for Age Restrictions

1. **Protecting Children's Privacy**
    - COPPA and similar laws regulate how online services can collect and use data from users under 13.
2. **Reducing Exposure to Inappropriate Content**
    - Age restrictions help prevent children from encountering content unsuitable for their age, such as explicit material, violence, or misinformation.
3. **Preventing Cyberbullying and Predation**

- Younger users are more vulnerable to online bullying, harassment, and exploitation.

4. **Encouraging Healthy Development**
    - Social media use at a very young age may interfere with emotional and social development.

Challenges with Age Restrictions

1. **False Age Claims**
    - Many children lie about their age to create accounts, bypassing the restrictions.
2. **Parental Involvement**
    - Some parents help their children set up accounts despite the restrictions, sometimes unaware of the risks.
3. **Platform Accountability**
    - Enforcing age restrictions is challenging due to limited verification mechanisms.

Age restrictions are an essential tool for promoting safe and responsible social media use among children and teens. However, their effectiveness depends on robust enforcement by platforms, proactive parental involvement, and educating children about the digital world.

How to Manage Child's Online Safety

Managing child' online safety is crucial in today's digital age. Here are comprehensive tips and strategies for ensuring they have a safe and positive online experience:

1. Educate About Online Risks

- **Open Conversations:** Discuss common online dangers like cyberbullying, predators, and inappropriate content.
- **Teach Privacy Awareness:** Emphasize not sharing personal details like full names, addresses, or school names.

2. Use Parental Controls

- **Device-Level Controls:** Enable parental controls on devices like smartphones, tablets, and gaming consoles.
- **Apps and Platforms:** Use child-friendly platforms with built-in safety measures and age-appropriate content filters.
- **Monitor Screen Time:** Use tools like Screen Time (iOS) or Family Link (Android) to set usage limits.

3. Set Clear Rules

- **Designate Online Hours:** Limit online activity to specific times of the day.
- **Approved Websites and Apps:** Create a list of pre-approved sites/apps they can use.

- **Supervised Usage:** Ensure young children use devices in shared family spaces.

4. Encourage Strong Password Habits

- **Unique Passwords:** Teach child to create strong, unique passwords for each account.
- **Password Confidentiality:** Instruct them not to share passwords, even with friends.

5. Foster Digital Literacy

- **Recognize Fake Content:** Teach them to identify phishing attempts, fake news, and scams.
- **Critical Thinking:** Encourage them to think before they click on links or accept friend requests.

6. Monitor Social Media

- **Understand Platforms:** Familiarize yourself with the social media platforms your child use.
- **Private Profiles:** Ensure their profiles are private, and they only connect with people they know in real life.
- **Regular Checks:** Periodically review their online activity and friend lists.

7. Teach Responsible Online Behavior

- **Cyberbullying Awareness:** Stress the importance of kindness online and how to report abusive behavior.
- **Content Sharing:** Explain the permanence of online posts and to think before posting.

8. Be a Role Model

- **Practice What You Preach:** Exhibit good online behavior yourself, such as limiting screen time and being mindful of privacy.

9. Encourage Open Communication

- **Safe Reporting:** Make them comfortable reporting anything suspicious or upsetting without fear of punishment.
- **Discuss Mistakes:** Address any online missteps calmly and constructively.

10. Use Protective Tools

- **Antivirus and Firewalls:** Install reputable antivirus software to guard against malware.
- **VPNs:** Use VPNs for secure browsing, especially on public Wi-Fi networks.

11. Regularly Update Knowledge

- **Stay Informed:** Keep up with the latest online trends, apps, and potential threats.
- **Community Resources:** Participate in workshops or forums about child' online safety.

By combining education, monitoring, and open communication, you can empower child to navigate the digital world safely and responsibly.

The Future of Social Media: Trends and Predictions

Social media is constantly evolving, driven by advancements in technology, changing user behaviors, and societal needs. Its future promises exciting innovations as well as new challenges. Here's what the future of social media might look like:

1. Rise of Immersive Experiences

- **Virtual Reality (VR) and Augmented Reality (AR):**
  - Social media platforms will integrate VR and AR to create more immersive experiences.
  - Users might interact in virtual spaces, such as metaverses, where they can attend events, shop, or socialize as avatars.
  - Examples: Meta (Facebook) is already investing heavily in this area.
- **3D and Holographic Content:**
  - Posts, calls, and meetings could become 3D or holographic, making digital interactions feel more lifelike.

2. Artificial Intelligence (AI) Integration

- **Personalized Content:**
  - AI will enhance algorithms to deliver hyper-personalized content based on users' preferences, moods, and habits.
- **Chatbots and Virtual Influencers:**

    - AI-powered bots and digital avatars will be increasingly used for customer service, content creation, and entertainment.
- **Improved Moderation:**
    - AI will play a bigger role in detecting and managing harmful content, misinformation, and spam.

3. Decentralized and Privacy-Centric Platforms

- **Decentralization:**
    - Blockchain technology may lead to decentralized social media platforms, where users have greater control over their data and content.
    - Examples: Platforms like Mastodon and BlueSky are already exploring this model.
- **Focus on Privacy:**
    - Stricter regulations (like GDPR) and consumer demand will push platforms to prioritize privacy, with features like encryption, anonymous sharing, and data ownership.

4. Increased Monetization Opportunities

- **Creator Economy Boom:**
    - Social media will further empower content creators with enhanced monetization tools like subscriptions, tipping, and token-based economies.
- **Virtual Goods and NFTs:**

- Users will buy, sell, and trade digital assets, such as artwork, virtual items, and NFTs (Non-Fungible Tokens), on social media.

5. Enhanced Interactivity with IoT (Internet of Things)

- Social media could integrate with smart devices, enabling users to share updates from everyday activities (e.g., health data from wearables or smart home activities).

6. Social Commerce Evolution

- **Seamless Shopping:**
    - Social media platforms will blur the line between browsing and shopping with features like AR try-ons, live-stream shopping events, and AI-based recommendations.
    - Examples: Instagram and TikTok have already integrated shopping features.

7. Rise of Niche Communities

- General platforms may give way to smaller, interest-focused networks, offering tailored experiences to specific audiences (e.g., hobbyists, professionals, or gamers).

8. Ethical and Sustainable Practices

- **Responsible Algorithms:**

  - There will be increased pressure on platforms to design algorithms that promote mental well-being and reduce addictive behaviors.
- **Green Technology:**
  - Platforms might adopt sustainable practices, such as reducing energy consumption in their data centers.

9. Short-Form and Ephemeral Content Dominance

- Platforms will continue to prioritize short-form video and temporary content (e.g., stories, reels), which align with shorter attention spans and demand for immediacy.

10. Greater Role in Society

- **Education and Activism:**
  - Social media will play a larger role in spreading awareness, educating users, and facilitating grassroots movements.
- **Digital Identity:**
  - Social media profiles may evolve into comprehensive digital identities, integrating credentials, portfolios, and social connections.

Challenges Ahead

- **Regulation:** Governments will likely enforce stricter regulations around content moderation, misinformation, and data privacy.

- **Digital Overload:** As platforms expand, managing screen time and balancing real-life interactions will remain a concern.
- **Misinformation and Ethics:** Ensuring accountability and accuracy in information shared online will be a key challenge.

The future of social media promises a blend of cutting-edge technologies, personalized experiences, and a stronger focus on user well-being and privacy. While it will create opportunities for deeper connections and creativity, it will also demand vigilance to address ethical, societal, and regulatory challenges.

Disclaimer

This book is intended for informational purposes only. The content within is based on personal experience, research, and best practices related to social media strategies. While every effort has been made to ensure the accuracy and completeness of the information, the author is not responsible for any errors, omissions, or outcomes resulting from the use of this book.

Social media platforms frequently update their policies, features, and algorithms. Readers are encouraged to stay informed about changes directly from the platforms.

By using this book, you acknowledge and agree that the author shall not be held liable for any decisions or actions taken based on the content provided herein. Use the strategies and advice in this book at your own discretion.

9 789334 301731

Printed at Repro India Ltd.